First Impressions

DATE		

SUSAN E. MEYER

Mary Cassatt

SERIES EDITOR: Robert Morton
DESIGNERS: Dana Sloan and Laura Lovett
PHOTO RESEARCH: Neil Ryder Hoos

LIBRARY OF CONGRESS CATALOGING-IN-PUBLICATION DATA
Meyer, Susan E.
Mary Cassatt / by Susan E. Meyer.
92 p. 19 × 25.7cm. — (An Abrams first impressions book)
Summary: Examines the life and work of the strong-willed American woman who studied in Paris and
became a noted contributor to the Impressionist movement.
ISBN 0-8109-3154-0
1. Cassatt, Mary, 1844-1926 — Juvenile literature. 2. Artists — United States — Biography — Juvenile
literature. [1. Cassatt, Mary, 1844-1926. 2. Artists. 3. Painting, American. 4. Art appreciation.] I. Title.
II. Series.
N6537.C35M49 1990
759.13 — dc19
[B]   89-443
[92]   CIP
Text copyright © 1990 Susan E. Meyer
Illustrations copyright © 1990 Harry N. Abrams, Inc.
Published in 1990 by Harry N. Abrams, Incorporated, New York
A Times Mirror Company
Printed and bound in Hong Kong

· Contents ·

To the memory of Lloyd Melnick

♦ **The Map**. 1889

1 ✦ Young Miss Cassatt

Mary Cassatt was twenty-one years old when she announced to her parents that she intended to become a professional artist. Once Mary made up her mind, there was no changing it. Even when her father cried out, "I would almost rather see you dead," she remained firm.

Six years earlier, when she had first decided to study art, her father had been very pleased. He was proud that his daughter wanted to attend the famous Pennsylvania Academy of the Fine Arts in Philadelphia, and he even accompanied her to school each day on his way to his downtown office. After all, studying the art of drawing and painting was recommended for respectable young ladies in those days. But it was one

This drawing of Mary Cassatt, her father, Robert S. Cassatt, and her brothers, Gardner (left) and Robert, was made by Peter Baumgartner in Germany in 1854, only months before Robbie died.

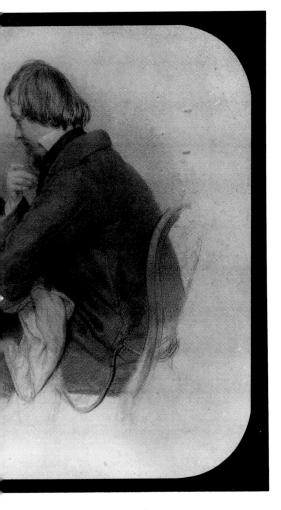

thing for a woman to pass the time by painting pleasing pictures, and altogether another thing to make a *career* out of this hobby! It was fine for her to paint flowers on pottery, perhaps, but not to work from live models in a dusty studio! But Mary Cassatt was different from other girls, and she knew it by the time she was fifteen years old.

If she wanted to succeed in her mission, Mary had to be different. Her willfulness, her single-mindedness, were personality traits that fueled her determination to become a great artist at a time when all the odds were against her. She did indeed become a great artist, famous for her oil paintings, pastels, and prints of mothers and children. This achievement was remarkable for any artist, but especially for a woman, considering that women artists weren't taken seriously as professionals. And it was also remarkable because she was an American, at a time when the international art world tended to consider Americans less cultured. Living in France all her adult life, Mary Cassatt was the only American to be invited into the group of experimental artists known as the Impressionists.

But Mary Cassatt helped to give American art more than self-respect. She was almost single-handedly responsible for introducing the paintings of the French Impressionists to the United States. Because of her tireless efforts, America has in its museums some of the finest examples of French Impressionism in the world.

In spite of her father's reservations about Mary's future as an artist, Mr. Cassatt never held her back. In fact, he may even have been responsible for her making the decision to become an artist in the first place, although he would have hated to admit it. He adored all his children, and he went out of his way to give them every cultural and educational opportunity. It's no coincidence that two of his children would eventually become famous. While Mary became a major artist, her brother Alexander was probably even better known as the president of the Pennsylvania Railroad at a time when the railroad was central to American life.

Although the Cassatts were by no means the most prosperous family in Pennsylvania, they led a very comfortable life. Mary's father, Robert, made some money in banking and real estate, but he was not aggressively ambitious, preferring to travel and to spend time with his family instead. He must have been a restless man, because he was continually changing his residence. He was born and raised in Pittsburgh, Pennsylvania, which was considered nearly the Far West when his own father had settled there many years before, and he continued to live in Pittsburgh after he was married. But by the time he had been married fourteen years, he had already moved the family into five different houses.

Mr. and Mrs. Robert Cassatt had five children: Lydia, Alexander, Robert, Mary (born in 1844), and Gardner. When Mary was five years old, her father decided it was again time to move, this time from Pittsburgh to Philadelphia; two years later, he grew restless again, this time moving the family all the way to Europe.

Mary Cassatt was seven when she saw Paris for the first time. After nearly two weeks on the ship crossing the Atlantic Ocean, and several hours on the train from the port to Paris, Mary approached the city with intense expectations. Imagine her excitement when she first beheld that great French capital. Did she ever guess that one day she would make her life there, that Paris would be more home to her than any American city? Probably not.

The family moved into a furnished apartment in one of the liveliest sections of Paris, near the great boulevard called the Champs-Elysées, where so many

◆ **Reading Le Figaro**. 1878

After first posing models artificially, Mary began to paint
everyday people in everyday settings. Here, she portrays her
mother reading a Parisian daily newspaper.

◆ **Alexander Cassatt and His Son Robert**. 1884–85

Mary's brother, known as Aleck, was a great financial help to the family
after their father retired.

interesting people strolled arm in arm or drove by in carriages drawn by handsome horses. The tree-lined streets and outdoor cafés, the city's sounds, the marvelous smells, were all new and exciting.

Paris was especially exciting in 1851, even for a young girl who knew nothing about politics. Louis Napoleon, who had been president of the French Republic, declared that France would henceforth be an empire and that he would now be called Emperor Napoleon III. These political changes were to set into motion many others that would eventually have a major impact on the art world in France and consequently on Mary's future as an artist, but for the time being she was aware only of the colorful parades and celebrations held throughout Paris.

Like other cultured young girls of her generation, Mary's mother had been taught French by a tutor when she was a child, and she was pleased to see her own children adapt to the language so quickly. Mary's brother Alexander was sent to a school designed to promote his talent for technical subjects, while Mary's other older brother, Robbie, was placed under specialized medical care for a bone disease in his knee. After two years in Paris Mary's father again uprooted the family, this time to Germany, where Alexander could attend a boarding school that would help prepare him for a career in engineering and where several medical specialists would study Robbie's perplexing disease.

The family remained in Germany for several months, hopeful that Robbie's condition would improve under the care of the specialists, but this was not to be. Throughout her life, Mary would shudder at the recollection of the time when tragedy fell early in 1855. The thirteen-year-old Robbie, unable to fight off the disease that had afflicted him since he was a small child, died quite suddenly. He was buried very simply in a local cemetery.

In grief, the family left Germany, passing a few months in Paris, then returning to Philadelphia, while Alexander remained behind in Germany to complete his studies. Mary was eleven years old. The time she had spent in Europe had made an indelible mark. When she returned to Europe years later, it would be to stay.

Although Philadelphia was certainly not Paris, the American city had much to offer in 1855. It was second only to New York as the largest city in the United States, and it was the fourth largest in the world. An important commercial city linking the East and the Midwest, Philadelphia was also a major cultural center, owing primarily to the Pennsylvania Academy of the Fine Arts. The Academy served as museum, art school, and a gallery attended yearly by thousands.

We don't know exactly when Mary decided to study art seriously, but we do know how eager she was to begin: she applied to the Academy in April 1860, a full six months before classes started and even before she was sixteen, which was the minimum age required for admission.

The Academy was considered modern because it admitted female students, although men and women didn't study in the same classes. The school was very different from today, and so were the students. The female students, for example, dressed according to fashions. (The trim, poised Mary was especially stylish and continued to dress fashionably until she was a very old woman.) It is certainly hard to imagine how a woman could work at an easel, dressed in so much fabric: the full, floor-length skirt ballooned out with stiff petticoats, the blouse pulled snugly at the waist, and the billowing sleeves extended to the wrists. Wearing aprons to protect the skirts, the female students worked side-by-side in the classroom, ignoring the globs of paint that stuck to the puffy sleeve or the plaster dust that the long skirt swept up from the floor.

While the Academy was considered progressive for admitting women, the coursework might seem dreary by today's standards. Classes aimed to train artists by developing their technical skills, not their imaginations. For the first two years an art student had to concentrate on drawing and anatomy exclusively—drawing white plaster casts made of classic sculptures, sketching other statues and live models, and attending anatomy lectures. The art student could decide to specialize in painting or sculpture after two years of drawing and anatomy, but not before. As rigid as it may seem today, this course of study was typical of all serious art schools, and especially of those schools in Europe.

Mary studied at the Academy for at least two years. During that time she made very good friends with her classmates, and was especially fond of Eliza Haldeman, who was also serious about pursuing a career as an artist and shared Mary's enthusiasm for the famous paintings brought over from France and England that were displayed at the Academy. Thanks to arrangements made by the Academy, art students also visited the homes of wealthy Philadelphia families that had recently begun to acquire paintings for their private collections.

Although Mary was acknowledged as one of the more talented art students at the Academy, she found her classes uninspiring. Rather than wait the required two years, she decided to learn painting on her own. She terminated her daily classes at the Academy, though she continued to work very hard. After two years she learned the basics of painting and mastered the technical skills, but she wanted more. She was determined to become a professional artist whose paintings would one day hang alongside the works of other great artists. By then it was clear that Mary had outgrown Philadelphia; the city was simply too confining for someone with her ambitions. Sad to say, no other American city was any better. In the 1860s art was still considered frivolous. Only in Europe would she find the opportunities she craved.

There was, of course, a certain snobbishness about Europe, a prejudice that America was merely a young, provincial nation, while the older European nations were more sophisticated. For a student of art, however, Europe's attractions were more than simply a matter of snob appeal. All the great masterworks were installed in the museums and churches of France, Italy, Spain, and England. The best art schools were there, too.

Once Robert Cassatt was reconciled to his daughter's decision, he supported her with all the enthusiasm he gave his other children. With her father's encouragement and blessings, therefore, in 1866 Mary made her plans for departure to Paris. A new life awaited her.

2 ◆ The Seeds of Change

◆ **Mr. Robert S. Cassatt on Horseback**. 1885

As soon as Mary arrived in Paris in the spring of 1866, she was struck by how much the city had changed since she had last been there. In those eleven years, many significant events had been set in motion by the emperor, the very same Louis Napoleon who had proclaimed himself Emperor Napoleon III in 1851 when Mary was a child in Paris. Mary was fascinated to see that even the way Paris looked was different from her memory of the city.

Napoleon had appointed his chief administrator, Baron Haussmann, to reconstruct the entire city, transforming Paris into the most spectacular capital in the world. The master plan called for grand boulevards radiating out, like the spokes of a wheel, from the center of Paris. Haussmann replaced the narrow, twisting streets and alleys with straight, gracious boulevards that were flanked by palatial buildings and shade trees and punctuated by spacious public squares and parks.

These visible changes in the city reflected less obvious ones in everyday life, changes that would have a major effect on Mary's future as an artist. France had grown far more prosperous in recent years. You didn't have to be a member of the royal family or even an aristocrat to afford a nice painting; now just about any middle-class family could purchase art to decorate its home.

Because so many people were eager to buy, art was becoming big business. More and more paintings were sold every year, which meant there were more and more artists, more and more art schools, more and more art teachers. For the first time there were writers called art critics who published their ideas in the newspapers and journals, informing the public about what was good and what was unacceptable in art. And now also there were dealers.

All this prosperity meant that an art student had a greater chance than before for a promising career. But if you wanted to achieve success in the art world, it was necessary to follow the rules closely and to advance yourself according to all the approved methods. The members of the Academy of Fine Arts established the standards for all the art being made and imposed them through their control of the enormous annual art exhibition called the Salon.

An artist could not succeed without exhibiting at the Salon. More than five thousand paintings might be submitted in any one year, with only half that number being accepted by the jury, consisting primarily of Academy members. Acceptance into the Salon was critical for two reasons: first, it meant that your work was "officially approved" and, second, it was likely that your work would be seen by many prospective customers and by all the Parisian art critics and dealers. A painting displayed in the Salon was thus more likely to sell.

But getting into the Salon meant following the rules. The jury would select only the subjects they felt were in good taste. They approved of historical subjects, pleasing pictures about everyday life, and paintings that told a story. Occasionally a landscape or still-life painting was accepted, but only if painted in a classical manner, the colors carefully blended, laid down layer upon layer in the tradition of the Old Masters. Dark colors were preferred to bright ones; drawing was more important than color. Originality was not encouraged.

Every spring the jury would work for days reviewing all the submissions. They would argue among themselves, fighting for their favorite students, trading one set of favors for another, until they had selected the more than 2,500 paintings for the exhibition. These paintings were displayed row upon row, from floor to ceiling, in the rooms of a large exhibition hall called the *Palais de l'Industrie,* which Mary Cassatt had seen for the first time just after it was constructed, when she was a little girl visiting the World's Fair in 1855. Every day during the exhibition, thousands of people would parade into the great halls of the *Palais:* the Salon exhibition was the biggest event of the art season.

Acceptance into the Salon required years of hard work. First you had to choose the right art school and study with the right teachers. Every promising young artist hoped to study with the members of the Academy who taught in the most prestigious art school in the world, the Ecole des Beaux-Arts (School of Fine Arts) in Paris.

Attending the Ecole des Beaux-Arts might be the best way to step onto the long ladder to success, but getting into the school was another matter. Competition was fierce. Those who failed the entrance examination, or who were ineligible for entry (such as women), had to study elsewhere.

Only a few years before Mary arrived in Paris, eight young artists had begun their careers according to the conventional rules, seven men and one woman who were soon to lead a revolution against the traditional approach to painting. They started out by studying in the right schools. The ones who were eligible applied to the Ecole des Beaux-Arts, and the others studied with established artists and schools. They did not start out as a band of renegades: in fact, they had hardly anything in common. Edouard Manet and Edgar Degas, the two oldest, both came from well-to-do Parisian families. Auguste Renoir, the son of a poor tailor, came from Limoges. Alfred Sisley was the son of a rich Englishman living in Paris, and Claude Monet had grown up in the north of France as the son of a grocer. Paul Cézanne was from the south of France, and Camille Pissarro all the way from the island of St. Thomas in the Caribbean. Berthe Morisot, the only woman, had traveled with her sister from the outskirts of Paris to study.

By the time Mary Cassatt came to Paris, they had all met each other, although they were not yet a tightly knit group of friends. A few of them had already begun to experience the frustrations of a system that discouraged their growth.

Manet was the first to attract unfavorable notice. At the beginning of his career, he showed real promise, actually receiving official recognition from the people who counted. Two of his paintings had been accepted by the Salon in 1861 and favorably reviewed by the art critics.

But Manet's popularity was short-lived. The following year, all three of his submissions were rejected. In fact, the jury rejected so many paintings that year that many artists protested. In response, the emperor agreed to hold a special exhibition, called the *Salon des Refusés,* for all those artists who had been turned away by the official jury. At this exhibition one of Manet's paintings, titled *Le*

◆ Self-Portrait. 1878

Mary painted very few self-portraits, and the one at left is special because it shows how her work changed when she decided to please herself rather than a Salon jury. Her technique became more free and she even experimented with different materials; here, for example, she painted with opaque watercolors, called gouache. At right is a photograph of Mary which she had taken during a trip to Parma, Italy, about six years before the portrait.

Déjeuner sur l'herbe (Luncheon on the Grass), created a scandal. In Manet's painting a naked woman is staring directly at the viewer, completely ignoring the two clothed gentlemen seated alongside her. Just what kind of picnic *was* this? Not only the scene, but the way it was painted appeared shocking. The oil colors just seemed to be thrown on the canvas, globs of paint heaved onto the surface. Manet made no attempt to blend the brushstrokes to achieve the slick, smooth surface favored by the artists of the Academy.

Manet found himself the leader of a debate between the younger artists and the old, established regime. The younger artists wanted to paint the world just as they saw it, spontaneously and rapidly. The older generation dismissed these paintings as unfinished, arguing that real art was meant to idealize the world, not

◆ Edouard Manet. **Le Déjeuner sur l'herbe (Luncheon on the Grass)**. 1863

Parisians were shocked by this painting when it was first exhibited. Not only was the subject thought to be indecent, but the bold, new way of painting was considered sloppy by the critics.

to reproduce it literally. Emotions ran high as the debates continued long into the night at the Café Guerbois, where many artists liked to gather after work.

Mary Cassatt could feel the fever in the air as soon as she entered Paris. Just how she would fit into all this would not be clear for a number of years, but the atmosphere of change surrounded her and she was affected by its force.

Mrs. Cassatt accompanied her daughter to Paris to see that Mary was properly settled. By the time her mother returned to America, Mary was living in the apartment of a quiet, respectable family that rented out rooms and served meals. Mrs. Cassatt could rest easily, knowing that other Philadelphia girls were staying there and that Mary would be chaperoned if she went out in the evenings.

There were plenty of companions for Mary. Her friend Eliza Haldeman arrived shortly after she did, and other students from the Pennsylvania Academy gave her an immediate circle of friends. The American girls tended to socialize only with other Americans from their own cities, and Mary was no different.

Where she was different from the others was in her seriousness about a career in art. As always, she refused to allow obstacles to stand in her way. Although the Ecole des Beaux-Arts was closed to women, she found several alternative methods of study. She received permission to copy paintings at the Louvre, the great French national museum; she attended the popular class given for women by a fashionable painter of the day, Charles Chaplin; and she took some lessons with Jean-Léon Gérôme, a highly respected artist who taught at the Ecole.

She soon found that the formal classes were not nearly as rewarding as independent study. By far the most inspiring source of instruction was the Louvre, where she worked long hours at the easel copying the paintings of masters she admired: the Italian Correggio, the Flemish portraitist Hans Holbein, and the great Spanish court painter Diego Velázquez. By looking closely at the effects these artists achieved with their oil colors, and by attempting to repeat these on her own canvas, Mary could explore different ways of handling the medium, training her eye and hand to translate what she saw into a convincing composition. It's as if the Old Master were there, leaning over her shoulder, whispering in her ear his secrets of creating the masterpiece hanging before her.

If painting in the Louvre inspired her to learn the secrets of the Old Masters, attending the Salon exhibition of 1866 must have awakened her to the developments taking place in art. Walking through the galleries of the *Palais de l'Industrie,* she must have had her first glimpse of a steeplechase scene by Edgar Degas. Another large canvas she must have seen was Claude Monet's life-size painting called *Camille,* which was the sensation of the exhibition.

While Mary found much to inspire her in Paris, she also regularly ventured into the French countryside for subjects to paint. Traveling with her friend Eliza Haldeman, she visited villages and depicted scenes of everyday life.

Mary was so encouraged by the results of her first year's work in France that she submitted a painting to the Salon of 1867. It was rejected.

Mary was in good company, for the jury had rejected many more paintings than they had accepted. Claude Monet was particularly distressed when his work was refused, given his success with *Camille* the year before. How could his work be accepted one year and rejected the next? "It is precisely because he is making progress that I am turning him down," sneered a member of the jury.

By then Mary herself was convinced that the system was in need of reform, but she persisted in pursuing the only route open to her. Undaunted by her first Salon rejection, she submitted another picture the following year, a canvas painted during one of her trips in the country. This picture of a young peasant woman seated pensively with a mandolin on her lap is a moody painting, revealing qualities she had learned from her work at the Louvre.

Before submitting *The Mandolin Player* to the Salon, Mary signed the painting "Mary Stevenson" (her middle name), rather than using her real family name. She suspected that the jury favored foreigners in their selection, and Stevenson sounded far more American than Cassatt. She may have been correct, because the painting was accepted.

The Salon was a great success for Mary. Although she didn't sell her painting, she did receive a nice notice in the *The New York Times*: "A portrait of an Italian girl, by Mary Stevenson of Pennsylvania, has obtained a place on the line, and well deserves it, for its vigor of treatment and fine qualities of color. Miss Stevenson has been a pupil of Gérôme, and proposes shortly to visit Italy."

After spending the summer in Rome, Mary was obliged to return to America at her parents' insistence. She probably would have stayed in Europe longer— forever, perhaps—if it hadn't been for recent events in France. Napoleon III had foolishly declared war on Prussia (now part of Germany). Mary set sail for America just at the time France was beginning to face a humiliating defeat. Almost as soon as Mary arrived in America she longed to return to Europe.

There was no hope of returning to Paris, at least for the moment. France was in chaos, Napoleon's precious empire destroyed forever. Parts of the beautiful city were now in shambles, having been bombarded during several bloody battles, and entire sections she knew so well lay in ruins. During the four-and-a-half-month siege of the city, the food shortage became so great that people were roasting their pets for meals. It was not until the summer of 1871 that order in

◆ **The Mandolin Player**.
1868
Mary's first successful entry at the Salon was this painting.

the city was restored, and this after many months of famine, plunderings, and executions. It would be quite some time before Paris was livable again.

Mary was determined to get back to Europe, even if she couldn't return to Paris. "I should jump at anything in preference to America," she declared to her friend Emily Sartain, a Philadelphia artist who shared Mary's enthusiasm for Europe. Mary and Emily decided they would travel together as soon as the first opportunity presented itself. Her parents agreed to cover her personal expenses, but Mary would pay for her own travel, materials, and models. She was a professional now, and her parents could not indulge her as if she was an amateur.

As it happened, Mary was offered a commission from a bishop in Pittsburgh to copy two religious paintings in Parma, Italy, by the great master Correggio. The commission would pay for her trip to Europe. "Oh how wild I am to get to work. My fingers fairly itch and my eyes water to see a fine picture again," she wrote to Emily. Two months later, during the winter of 1871, the two friends were on a ship for Europe. This time Mary was sure she was going for good.

3 • An American Artist Arrives

A detail of Correggio's **Madonna and Child with St. Jerome and Mary Magdalen,** painted in about 1523.

The small Italian city of Parma turned out to be an excellent choice for Mary and she felt at home almost at once. All around her were museums containing the works of Old Masters, and there was a friendly group of artists connected to the Parma Academy who immediately offered to help Mary and Emily settle in.

Having always been inspired by the work of Correggio, Mary welcomed the opportunity to study his paintings more closely. In copying Correggio, Mary had her first experiences in painting babies, a subject for which she would become famous. No one painted children as Correggio did. While the themes depicted in his paintings were religious, the scenes were always down-to-earth, and the models seemed remarkably similar to the people Mary saw all around her in Parma. Correggio's angels were not heavenly creatures, but real babies having fun.

Mary also studied the way Correggio handled qualities of light and shade, the effects of light playing on color. In his paintings the light seemed to be coming from the side and slightly above his subjects so that some of the forms were brightly lighted and others thrown in deep shadow. This dramatic effect, called *chiaroscuro,* created the illusion of real shapes, as if the figures were solid all around, not simply strokes of paint applied to a flat surface.

In Italy Mary was able to live and work quite comfortably on little income. A professor at the art academy helped her find a studio there free of charge. While copying the Correggios, she also painted pictures of her own choosing. Just outside her door she could find superb models, robust women dressed in colorful costumes, who were happy to pose for little money. (The cost of models in Parma was low even for Europe. In Paris, for example, Mary would have paid for one hour what a model there charged for an entire morning.)

In the autumn of 1872 Mary traveled to Spain, where she was thrilled to come upon marvelous paintings by the great Spanish masters Velázquez and Murillo. "I think one learns *how to paint* here," she exclaimed when she arrived. "I really never in all my life experienced such delight in looking at pictures."

The scenery and subjects were every bit as picturesque as she had heard, and she was soon painting toreadors, Spanish dancers, women dressed in colorful costumes and delicate lace, holding decorative fans. She painted so many canvases, in fact, that after eight months she had enough paintings for submissions to exhibitions in France and America for the next several years.

When her painting *Torero and Young Girl* was accepted by the Salon in 1873, Mary decided to leave Spain and go to Paris to see it hanging at the *Palais de l'Industrie.* She had mixed feelings about Paris. While she enjoyed the company of her many American friends living there, Mary was irritated with the established art world in Paris, feeling it was more conservative than ever. And she made no bones about her dislikes, which annoyed her friend Emily Sartain and eventually broke up their friendship. "She is entirely too slashing," Emily reported to her father, "disdains the salon pictures . . . all the names we revere."

It seemed to Mary that Paris had become more sober since the war with the Prussians. Yet, because the city was the center of the art world and because Mary was destined to be a prominent figure in that world, it was inevitable that she would eventually live there. But she was not yet prepared to settle down and decided instead to travel in Europe for another year.

In 1874 Mary found herself in a perplexing situation when another painting of hers, *Portrait of Madame Cortier*, was accepted by the Salon. She should have felt happy, but contrary thoughts kept nagging at her. No matter how many of her pictures had been accepted by the Salon, she knew that she would provoke the jury's disapproval if she gave in to her preference for experimental painting. Now that she was more confident, her brushstrokes were becoming freer. Her somber colors brightened, and she used a wide range of colors. No matter how she tried to convince herself otherwise, she preferred the spontaneous feeling of these energetic paintings to the static, sentimental pictures exhibited at the Salon.

Looking at her recent work, you would have to say that Mary Cassatt seemed to have more in common with those exuberant young artists, soon to be known as the Impressionists, who had just organized their first exhibition in the studio of a photographer called Nadar, the show timed to coincide with the Salon of 1874, where Mary's painting was hanging.

The idea for an independent art exhibition at Nadar's had been initiated by Claude Monet the year before. Artists who opposed the jury system and who were truly dedicated to "painting nature and life in their large reality," were invited to join an association they called *La Société Anonyme des Artistes, Peintres, Sculpteurs, Graveurs* (the Independent Society of Artists, Painters, Sculptors, and Engravers). The charter members included Edgar Degas, Claude Monet, Auguste Renoir, Alfred Sisley, Berthe Morisot, Camille Pissarro, and five others.

The exhibition at Nadar's included one hundred and sixty-five paintings by a total of twenty-nine artists. At first glance the style and subjects of these artists

◆ **The Family**. c. 1892

seemed so different—not only from the Salon work, but from one another's—that one wonders what they had in common. Degas, for example, painted the human figure, while Monet and Pissarro preferred landscapes. Degas was quite meticulous in his drawing and arranged subjects in striking compositions. With great precision, he painted methodically, placing layer upon layer of thin oil paint in smooth brushstrokes. The compositions of Monet and Pissarro, on the other hand, were loosely designed and the surfaces of their canvases were made rough by the thick paint piled up with short brushstrokes.

Regardless of their subject or technique, they had one thing in common: they recorded only what they saw before them. The real world didn't need improving. Even its defects were somehow beautiful. With almost scientific precision, the landscape painters analyzed how natural light, as it changed from one hour to the next, would actually alter the colors of objects. If you really looked closely, you would see that the colors in nature were very surprising: the grass might be a bluish color in the morning and a reddish color in the late afternoon.

Now that oil colors could be kept fresh in the newly invented lead tubes, these landscape artists were no longer confined to their studios. They could now pack up paints, easels, palettes, and canvas, and trudge out into the open. As they witnessed firsthand the wonders of natural light, they developed a new palette of bright colors and new techniques of applying their paint to the canvas. Using small brushstrokes and blurred outlines, they re-created the natural effects of "the beauty of the air in which objects are located," as Monet described it.

It was the group's obsession with reality that shocked the reviewers more than anything. According to them, this preoccupation with daily life and real people came at the expense of all standards of good taste. "They appear to have declared war on beauty," raged one reviewer. Another critic called the legs of Renoir's *Dancer* "as cottony as the gauze of her skirts," and termed Pissarro's *Ploughed Field* "palette scrapings placed uniformly on a dirty canvas. It has neither head nor tail, top nor bottom, front nor back." (This same reviewer was ridiculing the

◆ **Lydia at a Tapestry Loom**. c. 1881

artists when he called them mere "Impressionists," but the name eventually stuck to the group, even though it was originally intended as an insult.)

If the critics were unkind, the public was merciless. Throughout the halls of Nadar's gallery, outbursts of laughter could be heard as people jeered the paintings. The exhibition appeared to be a total failure.

Although Mary admired the work and courage of the Impressionists, she was torn by her ambition for success. These revolutionary artists seemed doomed. For years they had been working in isolation. Except for a small group of admirers and one dealer who supported them, they continued to be ridiculed by the art establishment and by the public. Some were even too poor to buy paints.

And so Mary deliberated. If she wanted to be a success as a painter, she would have to compromise. If she painted as she preferred, failure seemed inevitable; if she played according to the rules, she could expect rewards, but at what cost?

4 ◆ "Someone Who Feels As I Do"

Edgar Degas was walking through the Salon of 1874 with his friend Joseph Tourny. Not surprisingly, he found himself indifferent to most of the work crowded on the walls. In his view, the most interesting paintings of the year, including ten of his own, were currently hanging nearby at Nadar's studio on the Boulevard des Capucines.

Degas felt a kinship with the group because they were all united in their opposition to the jury system. Although he preferred to paint indoors, working frequently from memory, he shared his colleagues' obsession with depicting reality, moments of everyday life that were as fleeting as the landscapists' changing light. He haunted the streets of Paris to study the activities of modern life. As if he were looking through a keyhole, he painted the unguarded moments of performers backstage in the music halls, ballet dancers in rehearsal, jockeys at the racetrack, laundresses at work. Like the others, Degas examined the world around him. His figures were not historic; they were not dramatic; most of them didn't even seem posed.

Despite the indignities he suffered when the critics mocked the paintings on exhibit at Nadar's, Degas was convinced he had taken the correct route by exhibiting independently with the group and by vowing never again to submit to the Salon. He was still more confirmed in his judgments as he viewed the tiresome paintings hung throughout the twenty-four rooms at the *Palais de l'Industrie*. There were the usual heroic military scenes (always favorites with the public), the usual somber portraits, the same boring scenes from mythology and the Bible. Of course, there were also occasional exceptions, Degas admitted, as he paused to admire *The Railroad*, a canvas by his old friend and rival Edouard

Manet. But he was altogether unprepared for a painting called *Portrait of Madame Cortier* by the American artist Mary Cassatt. Here was a portrait of a middle-aged woman, a realistic portrayal that combined the techniques of the Old Masters with some very modern attitudes. After studying this painting for some moments, Degas turned to his friend Tourny and announced, "There is someone who feels as I do."

When Mary returned to Paris to live permanently in 1875, she dedicated herself to making a success, resigned to painting only pictures that would sell. She set aside her paintings of peasants the way a child sets aside her old toys. Instead she painted sophisticated women dressed in finery and portraits of well-to-do women and children. Working in this fashion, Mary achieved success almost immediately. Before long she was represented by a dealer in America and was receiving portrait commissions. After her first year in Paris she was living entirely from her earnings.

Detail of
**A Little Girl in
a Blue Armchair**

Meanwhile, Mary was making friends with other Americans, including one who would play an important role in her future. Emily Sartain introduced Mary to Louisine Elder, a nineteen-year-old American recently arrived in Paris. Louisine was overwhelmed by Mary. Eleven years her senior, Mary seemed so wise about so many subjects. She spoke with enthusiasm about art, about her experiences as a painter, about all the masterpieces she had seen. "When we first met in Paris," Louisine wrote about Mary many years later, "she was very kind to me, showing me the splendid things in the great city, making them still more splendid by opening my eyes to see their beauty through her own knowledge and appreciation. I felt that Miss Cassatt was the most intelligent woman I had ever met and I cherished every word she uttered, and remembered almost every remark she made. It seemed to me, no one could see art more understandingly, feel it more deeply, or express themselves more clearly than she did. She opened her heart to me about art while she showed me the great city of Paris."

From the outset Mary and Louisine were inseparable. As they visited the city's museums and galleries, Mary talked excitedly about the Impressionists. How she envied their vitality and originality and their courage! She found the work of Edgar Degas especially inspiring. "The first sight of Degas' pictures was the turning point in my artistic life!" exclaimed Mary. She told Louisine how thrilled she was when she passed a gallery on the Boulevard Haussmann and saw a group of pastels by Degas for the very first time. "I used to go and flatten my nose against that window and absorb all I could of his art. It changed my life."

Mary's enthusiasm for Degas' work was so great that one day she urged Louisine to purchase a pastel called *Ballet Rehearsal*. The $100 paid for it represented the beginning of Louisine's fine collection. It also represented the first time any American had purchased a painting by a French Impressionist. From then on Louisine would become infected with the thrill of collecting art. For the rest of her life she, and later her husband Harry Havemeyer, would look to Mary for advice about acquiring art in Europe. As a result of Mary's guidance, the Havemeyers eventually came to own the most important collection of Impressionist paintings in America.

In 1875 one of Mary's paintings (*The Young Bride*) was rejected by the Salon, while another was accepted. Louisine told a friend that she suspected *The Young Bride* was rejected for being "too original in style for these fogies to appreciate," and she was probably right. By this time, Mary's attitude toward the Salon had become quite cynical. She knew how to please the jury: she had only to follow the rules. And so she repainted the rejected picture, toning down the colors so that the background was darker and more somber. Sure enough, the repainted *Young Bride* was accepted the following year.

This incident may have been the turning point for Mary. Here was tangible evidence that the jury's taste was totally predictable and that she could win their approval only by sacrificing any originality in her work. Mary could no longer deny how much she had been compromising in order to win favor. She decided that she would continue to paint only along the lines that were true to her own nature, even at the risk of failure. A new era in her life was beginning.

By the time Mary and Degas met for the first time, in April 1877, Mary's family had come to Paris to live permanently. Mary managed to locate an apartment large enough to accommodate her parents, her sister, Lydia, and herself, while she continued to rent her studio nearby in Montmartre, the section of Paris where so many other artists lived and worked. It was to this studio that Degas came to call with Joseph Tourny, who had volunteered to make the introduction.

Their first encounter in Mary's studio was one of the most important events in

◆ *Overleaf:* **A Little Girl in a Blue Armchair**. 1878
In painting a child slumped naturally in a cozy chair, Mary had come a long way from traditional, stiff portraits in contrived settings.

her life. Older than she by ten years, Degas was a slight, round-shouldered man whose witty remarks often carried with them the sting of sarcasm. To people who knew him, he always seemed disgruntled about something or other, and he had become even more irritable recently. One of his brothers living in America had just lost the family fortune and Degas vowed to preserve the honor of the family name by assuming many of these debts. This decision meant that he was now forced to depend on the sale of his paintings, which distressed him. Selling was unpleasant because he was obliged to part with his works. Degas was a perfectionist, rarely satisfied with anything he painted, and he was always retouching his work. Even after signing a painting, he might scrape out entire passages and begin again rather than put it up for sale. He was actually known to buy back art that had been sold in order to improve upon it.

Despite his complicated nature, Degas could be extremely charming when the situation called for it. And there's no doubt that he must have been taken with this intense, talented, and forthright American woman when he met her the first time. He was very impressed by the work Mary showed him that day and offered to help in any way he could. They talked heatedly about the deadly consequences of participating in the Salon, and he urged her to do as he had done, to renounce the terrible system of juried shows and those hateful prizes that only encouraged painters to produce more mediocre work. By the time he left her studio later that afternoon, Degas had invited her to exhibit with the Impressionists. "I accepted with joy," Mary recalled years later. "I hated conventional art. I began to live."

Mary's meeting with Degas was the beginning of a tremendous creative outburst in her work. She would never again submit anything to a juried show. "At last I could work in complete independence, without bothering about the eventual judgment of a jury," she declared. Now that she felt liberated from the necessity of pleasing a jury, she began to incorporate more of the Impressionists' ideas into her painting.

◆ **The Loge**. 1882

Mary painted the scenes she saw around her, at home and in public places, like the theater and opera.

◆ **Lady in Black, in a Loge, Facing Right**. c. 1881
A print based on a drawing that Mary had made at the opera.

Mary had only one year to prepare herself for the next Impressionist show, and she lost no time in raising her work to their standards. Turning away from the contrived and artificial subjects she had painted before, Mary now painted her family and friends as they appeared naturally in everyday life: her mother reading a newspaper or a young girl slumped casually in a cozy armchair, for example. She no longer restrained her brushstrokes or toned down her colors to please the conservative critics. Now light colors, applied in free movements of the brush, made her subjects come to life. Mary felt she no longer had to work exclusively in the studio, now adopting the Impressionists' habit of making sketches on the spot. Wherever she went, she carried a sketchbook, ready to capture a spontaneous moment as it occurred.

As it turned out, the Impressionists' show was postponed at the last moment, which gave Mary another whole year to prepare. By the time the fourth Impressionist exhibition opened, on April 10, 1879, she had eleven paintings she felt worthy of showing.

In comparison to the other exhibitions, this Impressionist show was far more successful. Each exhibitor advanced money for the cost of the exhibition with the hope that the entry fees paid by visitors would cover these expenses. In fact, so many more viewers attended this time that the cash receipts at the door earned a small profit, which was shared by the exhibitors. (With her profits, Mary bought a painting by Degas and another by Monet.) Meanwhile, reaction to the show in the press was still unfavorable, except for some nice words about Mary and Degas: "M. Degas and Mlle. Cassatt are the only artists who distinguish themselves in the group of independents and who offer some attraction and some excuse in this pretentious show of window dressing and infantile daubing in the midst of which one is almost surprised to find their neglected canvases. Both have a lively sense of luminous arrangements in Parisian interiors; both show unusual distinction in rendering the flesh tints of women fatigued by late nights and the shimmering light of fashionable gowns."

In refusing to submit any longer to the Salon, Mary was prepared to sacrifice her greatest chance for success. But with reviews like this, she saw that she might still achieve recognition, even outside the official circles.

By now, even her parents had come to see that Mary was on the threshold of a promising career. Although they didn't understand much about this modern art, they were proud of their daughter's growing acceptance, and they wrote regularly to their sons in America, describing Mary's progress and enclosing newspaper clippings of her reviews. It seemed so long ago that her father had declared he would rather be dead than see his daughter an artist.

Over the next eight years—which has been called by art historians her Impressionist period—Mary transformed herself from a competent professional to one of the most original artists of her generation. There's no doubt that her friendship with Degas played a crucial role in her transformation.

◆ Mrs. Cassatt Reading to Her Grandchildren. 1880

When Mary's brother, Aleck, came to Paris with his wife, Lois, and their children, she found many new subjects to paint: here, Robbie, Katherine, and Elsie are pictured.

5 • The Impressionist Years

In many respects, Mary Cassatt and Edgar Degas were very different: Mary was vivacious, dynamic, and had a wholesome, optimistic view of life; Degas was given to dark moods, could be very cynical, and was often nasty. Yet, they also had much in common. Both came from families that respected literature, art, and music, and both were extremely cultured themselves. Above all, the two had similar ideas about art: they were committed to portraying their subjects truthfully and were convinced that drawing was at the core of good painting. Both preferred painting the human figure to landscapes and chose urban subjects over rural ones.

Degas tended not to pay much attention to women unless they were highly intelligent. In Mary, he found not only extraordinary intelligence but talent as well. It's true that Degas had been good friends with the gifted artist Berthe Morisot, but only about Mary did he say, "I will not believe that a woman can draw so well."

◆ Edgar Degas. **Mary Cassatt at the Louvre: The Etruscan Gallery**. 1879–80

For one of his prints, Degas depicted Mary examining an antique sculpture as Lydia looks through a guide book.

Degas may have also been drawn to Mary because she was American. His mother had been from New Orleans, and he had visited America five years before meeting Mary. Generally ill-at-ease with women, Degas may have felt more comfortable talking with this direct, outspoken American than with the French women he had known until then.

Like Mary, Degas was stubborn and opinionated, devoted to art to the exclusion of all else, even romance. We will probably never know for certain if Mary and Degas ever became lovers or talked of marriage, especially since she burned all his letters to her before she died. We do know that their friendship was well known at the time.

Degas showed Mary more kindness and generosity than he ever displayed to another woman. For example, although he despised pets himself, he went to great efforts to locate a Belgian Griffon puppy for her. For the rest of her life Mary always had one of these small terriers at her side.

◆ Edgar Degas. **Mary Cassatt**. c. 1884

Mary hated this portrait that Degas made of her. She felt that she looked ungainly and although she kept it for some time, she sold the painting right after Degas died.

But their relationship was very stormy. Over the course of their forty-year friendship, there were periods when they saw each other daily, other times when months went by without contact, and once she refused to see him for several years. To the degree that the forthright Mary was capable, she treated him tactfully in order to avoid provoking Degas' anger. But at times she would get angry at his behavior and then would refuse to see him. Once, for example, Degas made an unkind remark about Mary's work to a friend of Mary's. Mary was so furious at Degas that she would not see him for several months.

These eruptions continued throughout their long friendship. They almost seemed to enjoy the drama of their disagreements. "The state of their friendship was like a changing magnetic field," said one friend, "in which objects are given motion by attraction and repulsion. There were no tragedies or scandals. Their love simply grew into a part of the artistic life of Paris."

Although it was evident that Mary and Degas had intense feelings for each other, neither had anything to gain by marriage or a love affair. With Mary, Degas had the pleasures of intelligent and stimulating companionship. For the comforts of home he had his housekeeper, Zoe. Why should he forfeit his independence? Besides, he reasoned, how could he possibly divide his energies between love and art? "There is love and there is creative work; but a man has only one heart," he insisted. Meanwhile, Mary was probably too conventional to consider making a permanent relationship with a man whose way of life was so eccentric. And she was far too attached to her family and to her independence to change her ways now.

◆ **Susan on a Balcony Holding a Dog**. 1882

Like most of the Impressionists, Mary enjoyed painting outdoors. Here is one of the few times she painted a scene of Paris, a view of Montmartre from her balcony. She also included Batty, the Belgian griffon that Degas gave her.

As much as she revered Degas for his artistic brilliance, Mary pursued an independent course in her art. She learned a great deal from him, but she considered herself his equal, not his pupil. Their friendship thrived on mutual respect and a harmony of opinions. Never before had she connected with an artist whose ideas about painting were so similar to hers.

Although she was striving for a feeling of spontaneity in her painting, there was nothing spontaneous about how she created them. She shared Degas' opinion that "it is essential to do the same subject over again, ten times, a hundred times. Nothing in art must be left to chance, not even movement." Louisine remembered Mary talking about how hard she worked. Mary would say, "I doubt if you know the effort to paint! The concentration it requires to compose your pictures, the difficulties of posing the models, of choosing the color scheme, of expressing the sentiment and telling your story. The trying and trying again and again and oh, the failures, when you have to begin all over again! The long months spent in effort upon effort, making sketch after sketch. Oh, my dear! None but those who have painted a picture know what it costs in time and strength."

Mary and Degas were constant companions in each other's studios, each stimulating the other to try new methods. Degas was always experimenting with techniques, always developing new ways and adapting old ones. Pastel, for example, fascinated him. First introduced in the eighteenth century, pastel had been used exclusively for drawing, until Degas extended its range with his innovative ways of handling it. Because Degas was continually reworking his paintings, he was frequently frustrated by the fact that oil paint had to be scraped down and allowed to dry before it could be reworked. Degas was too impatient to wait; he also disliked the glossy surface produced by oil paints. Pastel offered him an exciting alternative. A dry, chalky medium that can be easily reworked, pastel produces a mat surface more like that of the Italian frescoes on the walls of the Renaissance churches Degas admired so much. There is no need to mix colors on the palette, as the artist is obliged to do in oils. With pastels, results are instantly achieved and can be just as rapidly altered, an ideal medium for Degas' temperament.

Degas devised a method of building up the pastel, layer upon layer, the way he did with oil paints, so that different colors would peek through the surface here and there. He developed a specially prepared fixative to spray over the pastel, which made it possible for him to apply another coat on top of it. Pushing pastel even further, he would spray water or even steam on it. Once moistened, the chalky pastel turned into a paste that could be pushed around with the tip of a brush. There were times when Degas would even grind up the pastel into a

The drawing above is a study for the painting **Five O'Clock Tea** (shown on the next pages) which was finished in about 1880. Mary also made an etching of the same subject. No one knows who the women are, but the setting is the Cassatt's Paris living room and the silver tea service is one the family owned.

powder, add water to make a "soup," and apply it to the paper with a brush. Mary tried all of these techniques and eventually developed her own methods, often combining pastel with oil paints and even with gouache, an opaque watercolor paint. Eventually she came to use pastel far more frequently than oil.

Mary and Degas also experimented with printmaking. She had learned something about engraving when she was in Parma, and now she became fascinated with the technique of etching, in which she drew an image on a coated metal plate and then burned out the lines with acid. The plate was then inked and the surface wiped clean, so that the ink remained only in the etched lines. Then the plate was put through a press and the ink transferred to a sheet of paper. For many years Mary dedicated herself to making prints, a demanding process that requires precision, patience, and control.

Mary's social life had taken as dramatic a turn as her work and she became well acquainted with several of the Impressionists. Although she became friends with Berthe Morisot, Eva Gonzalès, and Mme. Bracquemond, she realized she was different from these other women artists because she was not married to anyone connected to the artists' circle as they were, and she was not French. But she shared with them the unique position of being accepted as a professional woman in an art world dominated by men.

Mary also found herself leaving behind many of her conservative American friends. She continued to exhibit in America and would always proudly refer to herself as an American, but she had become identified with a group whose goals of portraying reality shocked many of her former acquaintances. Rather than mingle with American society, she and her family tended to keep to themselves.

For all her involvement with the avant-garde painters, Mary's way of life remained straitlaced. She even looked more like a Victorian lady than an artist. "Miss Cassatt's tall figure, which she inherited from her father," observed her friend Louisine Elder, "had distinction and elegance and there was no trace of artistic negligence or carelessness which some painters affect. Once having seen her, you could never forget her from her remarkable small foot, to the plumed hat with the inevitable . . . lace veil, without which she was never seen."

In the family, Mary's most constant companion was her sister, Lydia. Eight years older than Mary, Lydia was an ideal subject to paint, her distinctive features constantly a challenge, and she was always willing to pose. Lydia was also an ideal chaperone when Mary went to work in Degas' studio. (It was unthinkable that a young woman should go alone to a man's studio.)

Apart from the time she spent with her family, Mary worked day and night, driven by the thrill of seeing her work develop along lines that pleased her. Her output actually increased from seven paintings and pastels in 1878 to a record twenty-nine in 1880!

Mary's life seemed better than ever now that her work was going so well, and now that she and Degas were good friends and she had her family living with her. Although Americans seemed to have preferred her earlier, more conservative work, she was more accepted in France. She exhibited with the Impressionists in 1880 and again in 1881 and her work was being sold successfully through the Parisian art dealer Paul Durand-Ruel, who was a great champion of the Impressionists. She was also receiving good reviews, even in the conservative newspaper *Le Figaro* and the American paper *The Parisian*. How marvelous it was for her to see that success could be achieved without compromise!

Mary's life would have been ideal if it hadn't been for Lydia's illness. Her sister had been growing more and more frail over the years from a kidney ailment called Bright's disease, and in 1882 she died. Grief-stricken, Mary was unable to work for six months.

The same year her sister died, the Impressionists had a crisis in their midst that centered on Degas. The members of the group had become increasingly unhappy with him for wanting to bring in new artists they considered unsuitable; for contributing too little of his own work to the exhibitions; and for being arrogant about those who dared participate in the Salon, notably Renoir and

◆ **At the Theatre (Woman in a Loge)**. c. 1879

From Degas, Mary developed a fascination with pastel, and she came to use the medium even more often than oils. The subject here is her sister, Lydia.

Monet. One member of the group declared, "Degas has gone sour. He doesn't hold the big place that he ought according to his talent and, although he will never admit it, he bears the whole world a grudge. . . . Though he has great talent, he doesn't have great character."

By 1882 relations had grown very strained. Monet and Renoir were threatening not to exhibit with the Impressionists unless they could also submit to the Salon. Degas, in turn, refused to exhibit with the others if Monet and Renoir were allowed to participate in the Salon and if his friends were barred from the show. In the end Degas decided to withdraw. The seventh exhibition of Impressionists was eventually held that year and was even a great success, but Mary Cassatt and Degas were not represented. Ever loyal to her friend, Mary would not show with the Impressionists as long as Degas refused to participate. It would be four years before the group would agree to mount another exhibition.

These unfortunate events were further aggravated by a financial crash that occurred in 1882. Durand-Ruel, who had always purchased paintings by the Impressionists to support them, could no longer afford to pay the painters regularly. Trying to help, Mary lent money to the dealer and purchased pictures for herself and her family. Whenever she had the opportunity, she would send her American friends directly to the artists' studios, or the artists would drop off their paintings for Mary to show at her tea parties.

Mary also urged her now-very-wealthy brother Alexander to buy Impressionist paintings for his luxurious new home near Philadelphia, trying first to interest him in Degas' racing pictures, since he was passionate about horses. Alexander, not knowing much about art, was reluctant to acquire these strange paintings, but Mary persisted, insisting that someday they would be worth considerably more than he would be paying then. Alexander respected his sister's artistic judgment—and her business sense; he decided to purchase several paintings at her recommendation, eventually owning more than twenty.

If Mary had a good head for business, she was also sensitive about being

◆ **Girl Arranging Her Hair**. 1886

With this painting, Mary was able to prove to Degas that even a homely
model could be portrayed with style.

considered rich. She got angry whenever any of the artists carried on about her wealth. The truth was that her parents lived on a very modest retirement income and borrowed money from Alexander whenever they ran short. From the sale of her paintings, Mary paid for her own expenses—models and materials, clothes, and even riding horses. With her parents paying for living expenses, Mary still had some surplus funds, but never as much as the other artists thought.

Still depressed over the death of her sister, and burdened with these other troubles, Mary worked at a considerably slower pace. Her brushstrokes became more controlled and her shapes simplified. During this time she painted a portrait of her brother Aleck with his son Robbie and a handsome canvas of a girl arranging her hair, both of which expressed a more sober outlook.

In 1886, after much negotiation with Degas, the Impressionists finally agreed to mount their eighth exhibition. Mary was instrumental in these negotiations because she agreed to pay a good portion of the expenses for the exhibition in advance, for which she would later be reimbursed from the profits (none being anticipated, of course). Because of Mary's generosity, the struggling exhibitors would not have to reach into their own pockets to pay the exhibition expenses.

The exhibition was a letdown. Very few of the original Impressionists participated. The greatest scandal at the show was a huge canvas by the group's newest member, Georges Seurat. Entitled *Un Dimanche d'Eté à l'Ile de La Grande Jatte* (*A Sunday Afternoon on the Island of La Grande Jatte*), the entire canvas was painted with tiny dots of color in a technique called Pointillism. Mary had only seven paintings on display and Degas drew much criticism for a series of nudes.

This exhibition turned out to be the last time these artists ever showed their work together. Mary's excitement at being part of the group and the reassurance she experienced from sharing their goals were rapidly fading. Younger artists, such as Seurat and Gauguin, were the new revolutionaries and the Impressionists were going their separate ways. Mary was on her own now.

6 ◆ Maturity & Responsibility

As much as she loved them, having her family in Paris was an enormous responsibility for Mary. She was constantly juggling her time between working in the studio and tending to their needs. Her friend Louisine commented that Mary's life after the arrival of the Cassatts "was an example of devotion to duty! She held duty before her as a pilgrim would his cross. No sacrifice was too great for her to make for her family." While Lydia was ailing, Mary took time out to find places in the country to rent where her sister might be more comfortable. After Lydia's death, Mary's mother began to fail, suffering from rheumatism and a heart condition. Again, Mary would interrupt her work for long periods of time as she accompanied her mother to warmer climates in the winter, to southern France or to Spain.

For the eighteen years Mary tended her family, she never complained. She would get annoyed with her father, of course, because he was very set in his ways and would never admit to any weakness of his own, though he depended on Mary as much as her mother did. He would actually make fun of the women in his household, saying that Mary was "lamentably deficient in good sense about some things and unfortunately the more deficient she is, the more her mother backs her up. It is the nature of women to make common cause against the males and to be especially stubborn in maintaining their opinions about matters of which they are ignorant."

Meanwhile Mary went her own way, continuing to take charge of the family's concerns and ignoring her father's obstinate objections. If her father refused to take his wife's health seriously, Mary simply brought her mother to a warm climate without him. "I felt very badly leaving Father in Paris," she wrote to Aleck from Spain, "more especially as he evidently considered the whole thing perfect nonsense. He really cannot be made to understand that Mother is a sick

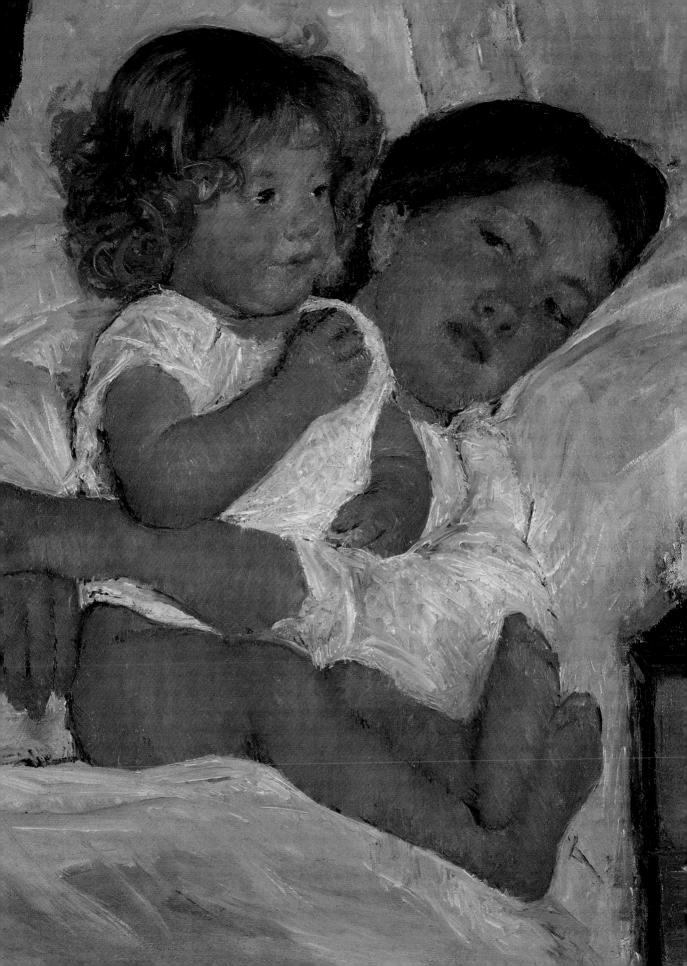

◆ **Breakfast in Bed**. 1897

In this painting Mary's technique of short, smudgy brushstrokes
resembles a work in pastel rather than oil, and she was clearly more
interested in subtle variations of white and gray than brilliant color and
pattern as in her earlier paintings.

woman and that if we want to keep her with us, she *must* be taken care of."

Not only was it imperative for Mrs. Cassatt to spend her winters in mild climates, her summers in cool climates, but also to have an apartment in Paris that was more comfortable than the five-flight walk-up they were living in. After much searching by Mary, the Cassatts finally moved in 1887 into 10 Rue de Marignan, just off the Champs-Elysées, near the center of town. The large apartment offered the luxuries of central heating and an elevator. A room off the salon facing north could serve as Mary's studio, so that she would no longer need to run the extra expense of renting a separate place to work. Even Mary's father had to agree that the new apartment suited them. A visitor who came to visit described the place this way: "It was stuffy and old-fashioned, very French Victorian — fringe on everything, lace curtains, heavy draperies with fringe, fringe on the lamps and tablecloths." On the walls hung the paintings by Monet, Pissarro, Manet, and Courbet that Mary had purchased.

By Parisian standards in those days, the household help was moderate in number. The Cassatts had a cook and a maid and a servant, in addition to Pierre, the coachman, who drove the horse carriage until he became the chauffeur once Mary owned an automobile. And there was a groom, of course, to tend the beautiful horses.

By the time Mary moved into the new apartment, the troubles of the early 1880s were behind her and she was working harder than ever. She was in her studio by 8:00 every morning and worked until the studio dimmed with the setting sun. She took tea every day in the salon and would entertain modestly, as she was an excellent conversationalist and had many interesting friends. Often she would work again in the evenings, on her drawings or on her prints. Only hard work would produce good painting: "There are two ways for a painter," she would say, "the broad and easy one or the narrow and hard one." There was no question which way she selected.

Mary's work was seriously interrupted again in 1888 when she had a bad fall from horseback after her spirited mount accidently tripped on the Champs-Elysées while she was riding with her father. She broke her right leg and dislocated her left shoulder. Degas came to visit Mary, even bringing flowers, and commented to a friend, "She is going on well, and here she is for a long time to come, first of all immobilized for many long summer weeks and then deprived of her active life and perhaps also of her horsewoman's passion." He was correct. Mary, an avid horsewoman frequently seen riding sidesaddle with her father in Paris' big park, Bois de Boulogne, never rode horseback again.

When Mary returned to work later that year, she began to focus on the subject that eventually made her so famous: the mother and child. She had already painted several pictures of children, primarily her nephews and nieces, and had actually been intrigued by the subject ever since studying Correggio's paintings of the Madonna and Jesus in Parma. Since the theme had recently regained popularity, especially among Americans, Mary decided to explore it further.

The subject of mother and child had endless possibilities and no matter what medium Mary worked in—pastel, oil, etching—she never repeated herself. Her happy children seem secure and loved in the laps of their mothers. Unlike the people in Degas' paintings, who are always so cool and distant from one another, the people in Mary's are always touching each other, delighting in the physical pleasure of being close.

Mary's paintings of mothers and children made an instant success when they were exhibited at the Durand-Ruel gallery. The critics loved them. One reviewer said, "For the first time, thanks to Miss Cassatt, I have seen the likenesses of ravishing children, quiet, bourgeois scenes, painted with a delicate and charming tenderness." Mary must have been pleased with this part of the review, but she was probably annoyed by another: "Furthermore, only a woman can paint infancy. There is a special feeling that a man cannot achieve. Only a woman can pose a child; dress it, adjust pins without pricking themselves." Mary, the professional on an equal footing with men, must have found these words foolish.

◆ **Gardner Held by His Mother**. 1888
Mary's nephew was often a subject for her drawings and paintings, as were most of the children in her family.

It's hard to imagine Mary ever having diapered a baby, but she certainly must have had a talent for keeping these squirming children amused while she made her drawings. Not that she didn't have her difficult moments, especially with members of her own family. One summer day, while the family was vacationing in the south of France, Mary painted her nephew Gardner, Jr. During the long painting session, the boy got bored and decided to put an end to the sitting by spitting in his aunt's face. Gardner's mother was so angry that she locked him in a closet for the rest of the day. Sympathetic with her nephew's plight, Mary went into town, bought a box of chocolates, and presented them to him as she let him out of the closet.

When her brothers and sisters-in-law and their children were not visiting France, Mary hired models to pose, sometimes with children, sometimes

◆ **At the Window**. 1889

Considering how many hours Mary spent working on each painting, it is hard to imagine how she captured such a fleeting moment between mother and child as is seen in this pastel.

without. She not only avoided any attempt to flatter these women, she actually came to prefer homely models, believing their imperfections made them more authentic. When she painted *Girl Arranging Her Hair* in 1886, for example, Degas had to admit the painting had real style, even though the model was downright ugly. Until then Degas had insisted that women were incapable of knowing what style was, but he was so impressed with this painting that he swapped it for one of his own and kept it the rest of his life.

Mary continued to paint every day, by now working almost exclusively in pastel. She also experimented a great deal with printmaking, turning to a technique called the drypoint print. A drypoint is made with a sharp needle scratched directly on the surface of a copper plate. There is no possibility of making any corrections, so one error can destroy the entire plate. "In drypoint you are down to the bare bones, you can't cheat," explained Mary. A friend noted the reasons Mary favored drypoint: "To impose on herself absolute precision in drawing after the living model, she chose this means of excluding all trickery and inexactitude. She was not satisfied to draw with a pencil. Instead she chose to use metal and a steel point so that the plate would hold every trace of her mistakes or corrections. Magnificent discipline!"

Mary's work took a real step forward after she attended an exhibition of Japanese art at the Ecole des Beaux-Arts in 1890. Both she and Degas had been interested in Japanese art for years, and Degas had already been adapting Japanese ideas into his work. Yet never before had so many items been brought together in one place. Overwhelmed by the display of more than one thousand woodcuts and illustrated books, the two artists returned to the exhibition several times and Mary purchased many prints for her collection.

The strong sense of line and the simplified shapes laid out in flat patterns intrigued Mary, as did the extraordinary compositions. Mary was particularly impressed by how many Japanese compositions were dramatically off-center and how objects in a picture were often abruptly cut off by the edge of the frame.

It was obvious that good composition did not depend upon placing the objects according to the traditional Western principles of harmony and symmetry.

Inspired by the masterworks of Japanese printmaking she had just seen, Mary feverishly set about executing her first prints in color. (She was so carried away with the Japanese prints that she unthinkingly drew the figures with oriental facial features.) Her prints were a great success. Degas agreed that they were among her best work. Flushed with excitement about her printmaking, Mary was eager to join a new association called the *Société des Peintres-Graveurs Français* (the Society of French Painters-Engravers), particularly since the group

Mary's prints were sometimes related to paintings but often began as original ideas. The print above, **Feeding the Ducks** (c. 1894), is based on **Summertime** (c. 1894) (see pages 2–3), but **The Letter** (1890–91), opposite, seems to have no precedent.

included so many of her Impressionist friends. She was dismayed to discover that she was ineligible to exhibit with them because she was not French. Neither was Camille Pissarro, who had come from the West Indies. To make it up to them Durand-Ruel organized a small exhibition of their work to hang in two rooms adjacent to the society's exhibition.

The collection of fourteen works on display in Durand-Ruel's 1891 exhibition was the first time Mary's paintings and prints were shown together as a group. Until then she had been rather modest about having a solo exhibition. But this small exhibition gave her a real boost, especially since Degas was so complimentary about her drawing skills, and she decided to prepare for another, larger show, with the eventual goal of exhibiting in America.

That year, the Cassatts rented a house in the country for the summer and Mary worked continually to prepare for her exhibition. By now her mother had grown accustomed to Mary's intense involvement with work, and she had even come to feel it was for the best, given that Mary was forty-seven years old and would probably never marry. She once wrote to her son that "a woman who is not married is lucky if she has a decided love for work of any kind, and the more absorbing it is the better."

But the summer did not turn out well. Her father, who had always been in excellent health, who enjoyed riding lively horses and walked six miles every day for exercise, complained the entire summer of feeling ill. After they returned to Paris that autumn, he died.

Mary deeply mourned the passing of her father. Her only consolation, as it had been in the past, was her work. She directed all her energies toward her forthcoming exhibition, and decided to make a major change in her life.

◆ **The Boating Party**.
1893–94

One of Mary Cassatt's
best-known paintings, this
large canvas is also one of
her most unusual: it is
probably the only mother
and child scene in which
a man is present. In its
style—the lack of fussy
details, the bold
composition, and vivid
colors—it demonstrates
the artist's fascination
with Japanese prints.

- ◆ *Above:* **Sleepy Child**. 1880
- ◆ *Right:* **Mother About to Wash Her Sleepy Child**. 1880
- ◆ *Next right:* **The Bath**. 1891–92
- ◆ *Page 72:* **Mother and Child**. c. 1890

No artist has ever depicted the theme of mother and child so successfully as Mary Cassatt. Starting with the early paintings of her nephews and nieces with their mothers and continuing for more than twenty years, Mary portrayed the subject in every form. Mother and child never seem posed; they are simply passing a quiet time together, and while the scene is always warm and loving, it is never sentimental or trite.

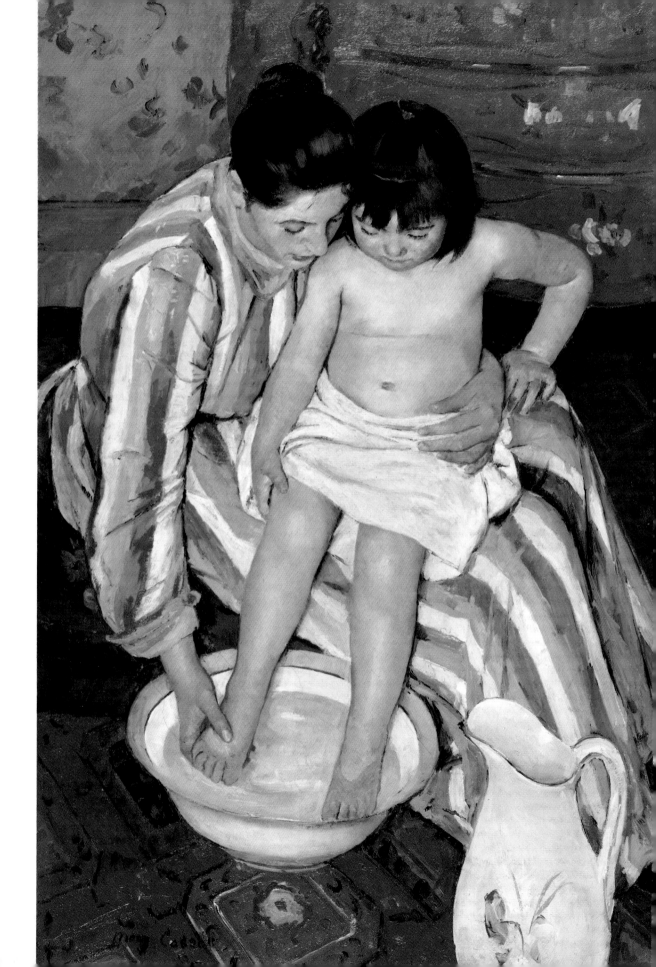

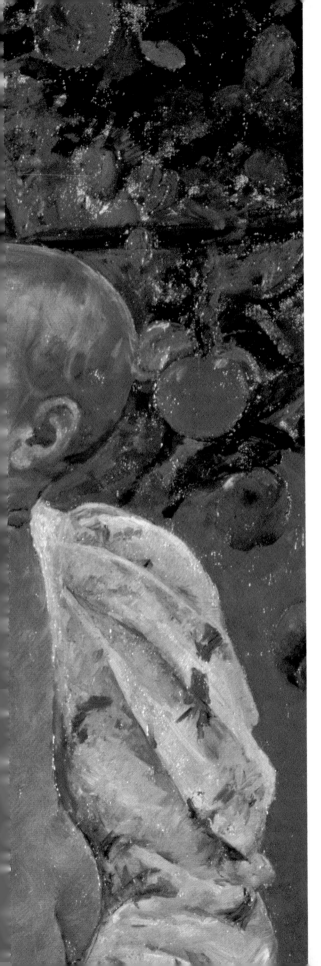

◆ **Baby Reaching for an Apple**. 1893

This is one of the many paintings and prints that were produced by Mary in preparation for the mural she was asked to paint for the Chicago World's Columbian Exposition of 1893.

7 ◆ Château de Beaufresne

B y the time Mary's father died, her success as an artist had greatly improved her financial situation. With her earnings she was now able to afford to buy her own home, and she decided to purchase an eighteenth-century house in the small town of Le Mesnil-Théribus. The home was called Château de Beaufresne or "Château of the Beautiful Ash Trees," because of all the splendid trees on the grounds. The pinkish-red-brick house was three stories high, with a band of white marble separating each floor. Located on forty-five acres not far from Paris, Château de Beaufresne allowed Mary to have a home in the country without giving up her Parisian apartment.

At the time she purchased it, the chateau was in a terrible state of disrepair, which meant that Mary and her mother could not move in until the following year, after all the renovation was complete. The timing suited Mary anyway, since she needed a year to work without the worry of moving. She had decided to undertake the most ambitious project of her life: a mural.

A great World's Fair was being planned for 1893 in Chicago. Among the many buildings being constructed for the event was a Woman's Building, which would celebrate the contribution of women to the world's civilization. Two wall paintings were to be installed beneath the building's enormous arches, forty feet from the ground. Mary was selected to paint the theme of "Modern Woman," and "Primitive Woman" was to be painted by Mary Fairchild MacMonnies, who is virtually unknown today, but at the time was far more famous than Mary.

Although Mary had never done a mural before, she was eager for the commission because she regarded this an opportunity to make a name for herself in America. It may seem odd that she was so much better known in France than in her native country, but there were many reasons for this. Until her show at Durand-Ruel the previous year, Mary had always been modest about promoting her work. Americans, and especially Philadelphians, seemed to favor her early work over her Impressionist paintings, and Mary was reluctant to subject herself to her compatriots' criticisms. She had a horror of seeming pushy, and she disapproved of artists who were too ambitious, like her fellow American painter John Singer Sargent. Moreover, she had consistently stuck by her earlier decision not to participate in juried shows or to accept any awards. She would have been better known, too, if she had traveled to America more frequently, but her family responsibilities kept her close to home. Now, she felt ready to advance her work in America. She could paint the mural in France and achieve the recognition at the World's Fair in Chicago.

But the assignment was overwhelming. Until that point, Mary had done only intimate scenes on a small scale. Suddenly she was faced with a monumental subject to be painted on a canvas twelve feet high by fifty-eight feet long. The first thing she did was to have a glass-roofed building constructed at the home they had rented that summer. She had a trench excavated in the ground so that, with winches, she could lower the canvas into it. This system meant that she could work on the upper part without having to climb a scaffold.

With great enthusiasm Mary started to paint in the early summer of 1892. But

◆ The mural **Modern Woman**, painted for the World's Columbian Exposition, Chicago. 1893

the effort was harder than she anticipated. Working every day for several months, she often became discouraged. She had hired several models and posed them in the studio for long hours through the heat of the summer and into the chilly days of winter, not letting up until the February deadline.

Mary developed a number of paintings and prints from her preparatory drawings for the mural, which was a good thing, because the mural itself was a great disappointment. Determined to work independently, Mary flatly refused to submit any sketches to the Fair officials along the way, and no one had any idea of what she was doing until the painting was nearly completed. Only then did they see that her mural clashed with the other one and with the rest of the decoration in the building. Once the mural was in place beneath the arches of the building, more than forty feet from the ground, it was impossible to see the figures Mary had labored over for so many months. One critic called the mural "unduly conspicuous," another said it was "more or less ridiculous," "somewhat inaccurate," and worst of all, "erratic." We will never know if the critics were correct for the mural was lost, or destroyed, after the close of the exposition.

Undaunted by her poor showing with the mural, Mary was now determined to make a name for herself in America with a solo exhibition. She immediately

◆ **Child with Red Hat**. 1901

In later years, Mary turned almost exclusively to pastel and developed a greater interest in portraits of children.

set out to prepare for a show that would open at Durand-Ruel's Parisian gallery and then move to his new gallery in New York City.

By the following summer, she had moved into her prized Château de Beaufresne. It was exciting for Mary to be living in her own home, actually purchased with her own earnings. She decorated the place with her favorite paintings by Monet, Pissarro, Degas, and Cézanne and with nearly one hundred Japanese prints from her collection. Her studio (or "painting room," as she called it) was located on the ground floor, with its windows overlooking the gracious lawn.

The grounds surrounding the chateau were Mary's pride and joy. She grew fruit trees and vegetables and planted over one thousand roses. Every day during the summer, Mary would place a large sun hat on her head, trudge out onto the grounds and tend her magnificent rose garden. She must have had a magical touch with the plants because it is said that no one has ever been able to grow a single rose on the property since Mary Cassatt lived at Beaufresne.

At the chateau Mary worked feverishly to prepare for her solo exhibition. The response to the 1893 Durand-Ruel show was thrilling. On display was a sizable collection of her most recent works, seventeen paintings, fourteen pastels, and about sixty prints. Several of the prints and paintings were derived from the sketches for her mural. Her work was praised by the critics, and the French government even requested one painting for its permanent collection of modern art at the *Palais du Luxembourg*. "No painter has seen with so much feeling," exclaimed one reviewer, "nor has anyone, with such convincing art, translated into canvas the poem of the family." People were saying that she was the most important American artist in Europe, at least on a level with James McNeill Whistler, the great American painter then living in London.

With a burst of enthusiasm, Mary made some new paintings to include in the exhibition when it traveled to America. She painted one of her most important oils, *The Boating Party,* a scene of a mother and child seated in a boat being rowed by a man. The bold colors, flat shapes, and dramatic composition express her confidence, her maturity, her independence. Mary's powers were at their peak.

It seems astonishing that Mary, by then so celebrated in France, still failed to impress the American public. Her New York City exhibition in April 1895 turned out to be a great disappointment. Few people attended the exhibition and the reviews were unflattering. *The New York Times* called her work "uneven" and "frequently hard, crude." Some reviewers seemed to resent her strength as an artist, suggesting that her work lacked "feminine delicacy." Except for the two paintings purchased by Louisine Havemeyer, sales were poor. "I am very much disappointed that my compatriots have so little liking for my work," she confessed to a friend. "Give me France," she declared. "Women do not have to fight for recognition here if they do serious work." But no matter how she rationalized it, she continued to feel hurt by the American rejection.

The year 1895 had turned out to be a very difficult one. Mary's mother became critically ill and was bedridden for several months. During the summer, Louisine Havemeyer came with her children to stay with Mary and to help care for Mrs. Cassatt. "In her last illness," wrote Louisine in her memoirs, "I recall sitting beside her, holding her thin hand in mine, filled with pity for the poor sufferer." Mary's mother died that autumn.

For eighteen years Mary had tended her family, and now that Lydia, her mother, and father were gone, Mary was alone. "To poor Miss Cassatt the loss was irreparable," remembered Louisine. "For years she put ambition aside to devote herself to her invalided family, and only when she laid them to rest in the quiet town at Mesnil, did she again return to work and seek consolation in her art."

For the first time in eighteen years Mary had only herself to think of. She was free to do anything she wanted. After all, at fifty-one she could hardly be considered a very old lady. She still had many years ahead, with many things to accomplish. But for Mary the passing of her family was the end of an era, not the beginning of a new one. Now that she had no one to care for, Mary's life no longer had the same meaning. She was never quite the same again.

◆ **The Caress**. 1902

This painting was selected for a prize by the Pennsylvania Academy of the Fine Arts, but Mary turned it down, remaining true to her principles, "no jury, no medals, no awards."

8 ◆ A Nation Enriched

◆ **Portrait of Mrs. Havemeyer and Her Daughter Electra**. 1895

The summer Louisine Havemeyer passed at Château de Beaufresne in 1895 was the first time the two friends had been reunited for a while. Busy raising a family while her husband was running his highly successful sugar refining business, Louisine had not been free to travel to Europe regularly. Now that the children were older and Harry was eager to embellish their two magnificent new homes in New York City and Connecticut, she planned to come to Europe more frequently to buy paintings.

Both Havemeyers were passionate about collecting art. Even before they were married, Harry and Louisine had each been collecting for years, though they had each developed very different tastes and habits. Harry was fond of antique Oriental textiles, porcelains, and other artifacts. He bought things impulsively and quickly paid any price that was quoted if he felt the work merited it. Louisine was less extravagant and liked to bargain. She preferred contemporary art, having been educated by Mary to appreciate the Impressionists long before other Americans had any taste for them. Unlike her husband, Louisine was patient, prepared to wait for years if necessary to acquire a good painting at the right price. It was their differences in taste and temperament that inspired them to build an unusually diverse art collection.

Mary, too, had been actively involved in advising art collectors since that day, long ago, when she persuaded Louisine to purchase the Degas pastel. For twenty years Mary persistently and passionately urged other Americans to buy works by the French Impressionists. She had two good reasons for her dedication: first, she knew the artists needed the money to survive, and secondly, she was convinced that America needed to be rescued from cultural ignorance.

Determined to elevate the status of art in America, Mary maintained that art should not be regarded as a luxury but an absolute necessity in life. After all, she insisted, Americans were rich enough to surround themselves with the very best money could buy. With the serious investment of wealthy collectors, America could emerge as the most important art center in the world. "All the pictures privately bought by rich Americans," Mary predicted, "will eventually find their way into public collections and enrich the nation and the national taste."

And so Mary urged all her friends and relatives to purchase art in Europe while there were still bargains to be had. (She was very generous—never taking a penny from the collectors for her time, and always willing to lend money to her artist friends when they were strapped—but she was shrewd in business and would recommend a painting only if she got the best possible price.) When she

◆ **Sleepy Baby**. 1910
As Mary's vision began to
fail, her paintings became
more vivid, sometimes
almost garish in color.

wasn't tending her family or working, she would be dashing off to Durand-Ruel's
gallery, or to her friends' studios, or to auctions in search of paintings.

Little by little, the Impressionists were coming into fashion with Americans—
through no small effort by Mary Cassatt. Her brother Alexander had purchased
several paintings at Mary's recommendation and he encouraged associates of his
at the Pennsylvania Railroad to consult her about investing in the Impressionists.
Other Americans who sought her advice included her cousin Annie Riddle
Scott, the Popes, the Hammonds, and the Whittemores. One American, a
wealthy banker named James Stillman, came to Mary for advice about collecting
art and eventually fell in love with her. They may have discussed marriage, but
Mary seems to have steered clear of any permanent attachment. She was in her
fifties, six years older than Stillman, and not likely to change her ways. Neverthe-

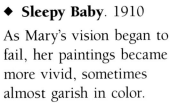

less, she continued a close friendship with him for many years and under her tutelage James Stillman became a connoisseur of fine European painting.

When the Havemeyers came to Europe in 1895, Harry asked Mary to help him locate Impressionist paintings, and Mary happily agreed. Louisine was thrilled that her husband was finally taking an active interest in the Impressionists, especially when Mary could use a distraction from the loss of her mother.

From that point on, Mary divided her time between painting and helping the Havemeyers amass one of the most important private collections in the world. As "godmother" to the collection, Mary was totally consumed by the task of locating the best paintings at the best price for the Havemeyers. In her quest she managed to find masterpieces not only by the Impressionists but by the Old Masters as well. Louisine would say that her friend "had the 'flair' of an old hunter." Mary visited the galleries frequently, inquiring as she entered, "Do you have any pictures for the Havemeyers?" She would negotiate the prices on behalf of the Havemeyers and act as a go-between on many transactions.

During this period Mary found time for her own painting, too. Although she frequently painted her favorite subject, mother and child, she found herself drawn more and more to children, and was becoming known for her children's portraits. She almost never worked in oils these days, preferring the rich colors and decorative effects she achieved with pastel.

In 1899 Mary traveled to America, her first trip in twenty years. Everywhere she went she charmed people with her lively conversation and fascinating stories about the Impressionists. The trip was capped with an unexpected triumph. She finally received a good response to a small exhibition of her work that Durand-Ruel had mounted in New York. One reviewer wrote that Mary "despises prettiness; but though some of her models might be called ugly, all are full of life and vigor, and no one can deny that she makes beautiful pictures of even the most commonplace." Finally Americans were beginning to take note of Mary.

All of us have benefited from the friendship between Mary Cassatt and the

In 1910, Mary (at far right) was photographed at the French palace at Versailles by James Stillman with her brother, Gardner, and his wife and two of their children.

At left, she is seen in 1914, wearing a familiar large hat and dressed fashionably, but conservatively. Mary disliked being photographed and this is one of the few pictures of her late in her life.

Havemeyers. Like Mary, the Havemeyers were dedicated to enriching America with fine art, and just as Mary predicted, the pictures eventually did find their way into public collections. When Louisine Havemeyer died, she bequeathed most of her fine collection to The Metropolitan Museum of Art in New York, where we can all enjoy her great legacy. The words "H. O. Havemeyer Collection" placed alongside any of these paintings can still evoke the image of Mary, Harry, and Louisine as they beheld the painting for the first time, thrilled and triumphant, and feeling as if they were plunging into an exciting new adventure.

Mary Cassatt lived to be eighty-two years old. By the time she died she achieved every goal she set out to attain. She lived long enough to see her art finally earn the high standing in America it had already enjoyed in France. She could look to the great collections of European art in America and take pride in the role she had played in building these collections. During her lifetime she was offered every conceivable award, most of which she refused, ever true to the pledge she had made when she joined the Impressionists so many years before.

All this fame came late in Mary's life. If she hadn't been so modest about promoting herself, she might have seen it happen earlier, but Mary was always reluctant to advance her work in public. She refused, for example, to have her name included among the list of exhibitors on the posters announcing the Impressionist exhibitions, feeling that it was in poor taste for a woman to display her name on billboards. And whenever the conversation among her friends turned to the subject of art, she spoke intelligently and with passion, but always seemed to avoid discussing her own work.

A friend of hers, the famous art dealer Ambroise Vollard, once told a story about Mary that illustrated her extreme modesty. He and Mary were attending an exhibition of the Impressionists in Paris and overheard two women arguing. One woman turned to Mary without knowing who she was and said, "But you are forgetting a foreign painter who Degas thinks is first rate."

"Who is that?" Mary asked in astonishment.

"Mary Cassatt."

"Oh, nonsense," Mary exclaimed, without false modesty.

"She's jealous," murmured the other woman, turning away.

Considering how sensitive Mary was about seeming aggressive, it must have pleased her when, on two occasions, she felt she could accept recognition without compromising her principles. One award especially gratified her, the distinguished *Légion d'honneur* presented to her in 1904 by the French government. That such an honor was bestowed on a woman, especially an American woman, was extraordinary. She was so proud of the award that for a full year she regularly wore the *Légion's* distinctive red ribbon pinned to her collar. Mary also made an exception to her rules by accepting the Gold Medal of Honor awarded by her old school, the Pennsylvania Academy of the Fine Arts. She was honored not only for her achievements as an artist, but also for her role in bringing so much fine European art to America.

Within two years of Mary's death in 1926, four memorial exhibitions of her work were mounted in the United States. The largest of these presented over forty paintings and pastels, fifteen drawings and watercolors, and one hundred prints created by Mary during her lifetime. She would have been pleased by this review: "Not until now has there been afforded the opportunity to realize how varied was her accomplishment, and under what sundry influences she worked, though at all times maintaining her own individual style."

What would have pleased Mary most of all was that this exhibition and review appeared in her home town of Philadelphia. Mary Cassatt, who had ventured so far in an uncharted frontier, was home at last.

• List of Illustrations •

Pages 48–49
Five O'Clock Tea. c. 1880
Oil on canvas, 25½ × 36½". Museum of Fine
Arts, Boston. M. Theresa B. Hopkins Fund

Page 52
At the Theatre (Woman in a Loge). c. 1879
Pastel on paper, 21¹³⁄₁₆ × 18⅛".
The Nelson-Atkins Museum of Art, Kansas City.
Acquired through the generosity of an
anonymous donor

Page 54
Girl Arranging Her Hair. 1886
Oil on canvas, 29½ × 24½". National Gallery of
Art, Washington, D.C. Chester Dale Collection

Page 57
Detail of *Breakfast in Bed.*

Page 58
Breakfast in Bed. 1897
Oil on canvas, 23 × 29".
Henry E. Huntington Library and Art Gallery.
The Virginia Steele Scott Collection

Page 61
Gardner Held by His Mother. 1888
Drypoint, 8¼ × 5⁷⁄₁₆". S. P. Avery Collection,
Miriam and Ira D. Wallach Division of Art, Prints
and Photographs. The New York Public Library
Astor, Lenox and Tilden Foundations

Page 62
At the Window. 1889
Pastel and charcoal on gray paper, 29¾ × 24½".
Musée du Louvre, Paris

Page 64
Feeding the Ducks. c. 1894
Drypoint and aquatint on three plates, third state,
15 × 20⅛". Terra Museum of American Art,
Chicago. Daniel J. Terra Collection

Page 65
The Letter. 1890–91
Color print with drypoint and aquatint,
13¹¹⁄₁₆ × 9". National Gallery of Art, Washington,
D.C. Chester Dale Collection

Pages 67–68
The Boating Party. 1893–94
Oil on canvas, 35½ × 46⅛".
National Gallery of Art, Washington, D.C. Chester
Dale Collection

Page 69
Sleepy Child. 1880
Pastel, 24⅜ × 18¼". Collection Antonette and
Isaac Arnold, Jr., Houston

Page 70
Mother About to Wash Her Sleepy Child. 1880
Oil on canvas, 39½ × 25¾".
The Los Angeles County Museum of Art. Mrs.
Fred Hathaway Bixby Bequest

Page 71
The Bath. 1891–92
Oil on canvas, 39½ × 26".
The Art Institute of Chicago. Robert Waller Fund

Page 72
Mother and Child. c. 1890
Oil on canvas, 35⅜ × 25⅜". Wichita Art
Museum, the Roland P. Murdock Collection

Pages 73–74
Detail of *Baby Reaching for an Apple.*

Page 74
Baby Reaching for an Apple. 1893
Oil on canvas, 39½ × 25¾". Virginia Museum of
Fine Arts, Richmond. Gift of an Anonymous
Donor

Pages 76–77
Modern Woman (mural at the World's Columbian
Exposition). 1893
Oil on canvas, 12 × 58'.
Chicago Historical Society

Page 78
Child with Red Hat. 1901
Pastel on paper, 20¾ × 17⅛".
Sterling and Francine Clark Art Institute,
Williamstown, Massachusetts

Page 81
The Caress. 1902
Oil on canvas, 32⅞ × 27⅜". National Museum of
American Art, Smithsonian Institution,
Washington, D.C. Gift of William T. Evans

Page 82
*Portrait of Mrs. Havemeyer and Her Daughter
Electra.* 1895
Pastel on paper, 24 × 30½".
Private Collection

Page 84
Sleepy Baby. 1910
Pastel, 25½ × 20½".
Dallas Museum of Fine Arts. Munger Fund

Page 85
Detail of *Sleepy Baby.*

Page 87 (top and bottom)
Photographs of Mary Cassatt.
Frederick Arnold Sweet papers, Archives of
American Art, Smithsonian Institution,
Washington, D.C.

◆ Index ◆